Let's Comm

by Elizabeth Moore

Consultant:
Adria F. Klein, Ph.D.
California State University, San Bernardino

capstone
classroom

Heinemann Raintree • Red Brick Learning
division of Capstone

We communicate in many different ways.

We communicate when we talk and write.

We talk with family.

We talk when we play games together.

We talk with friends.

We talk with friends on the phone.

We send letters to friends.

Sending letters is a way to communicate.

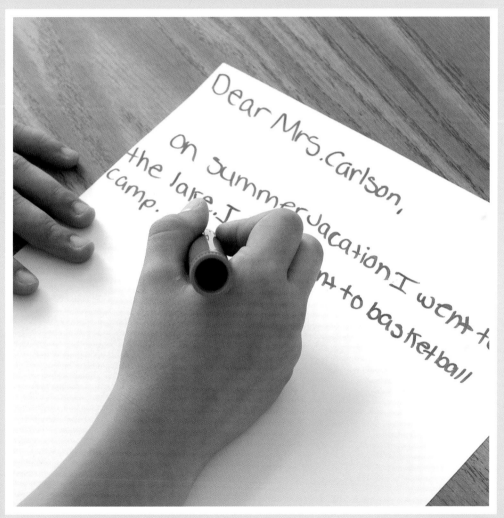

We send emails to friends.

Emails are a way to communicate.

Sometimes people use sign language.

Using sign language is a way to communicate.

Sometimes people use signs.

STOP

SCHOOL SAFETY PATROL

Using signs is a way to communicate.

How do you communicate?